FIND OUT ABOUT
PLASTIC

© 1994 Watts Books

Watts Books
96 Leonard Street
London EC2A 4RH

Franklin Watts Australia
14 Mars Road
Lane Cove
NSW 2066

UK ISBN: 0 7496 1591 5

10 9 8 7 6 5 4 3 2 1

Dewey Decimal Classification 668.4

A CIP catalogue record for this book
is available from the British Library

Editor: Annabel Martin
Design: Thumb Design
Cover design: Chloë Cheesman

Additional photographs:
Royal Botanical Gardens,
Kew/Courtaulds 9, 19;
© Tony Stone Worlwide 18.

Printed in Hong Kong

FIND OUT ABOUT
PLASTIC

Henry Pluckrose

Photography by Chris Fairclough

Watts Books

London • New York • Sydney

These garden tools ...

these bags and bottles . . .

this cyclist's clothing ...

and these bags which hold tea
have something in common.
They are made with material
which has been manufactured
in a factory.
These man-made materials
did not grow naturally —
like wool on a sheep
or cotton on a plant.

About 100 years ago, scientists discovered that if they soaked tiny pieces of wood in chemicals they could spin a fine thread from the mixture.

They had discovered cellulose.

Cellulose is soft.
It absorbs water.
We use it to make nappies.

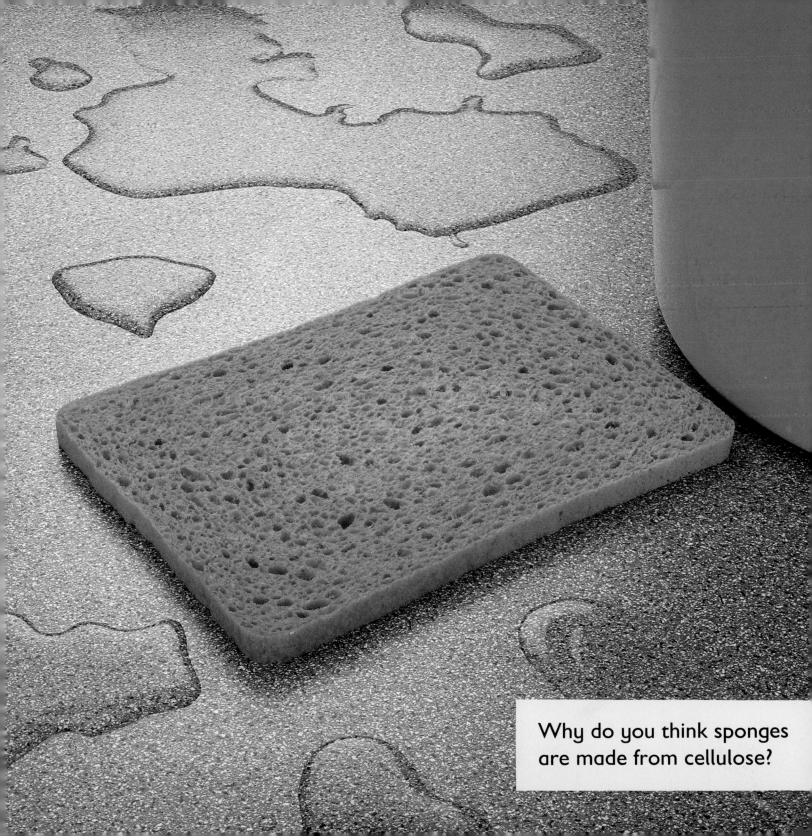

Why do you think sponges are made from cellulose?

Cellulose is very tough.
It is used to give extra strength
to tyres ...

and to make paper wrappings
for food and sweets.
Is cellophane easy to tear?

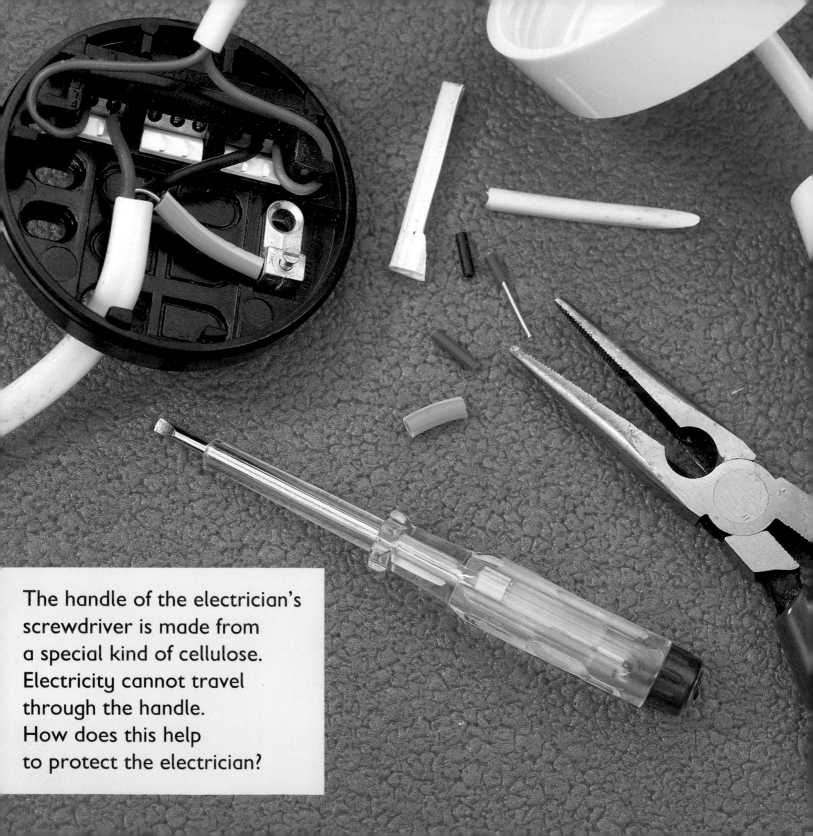

The handle of the electrician's screwdriver is made from a special kind of cellulose. Electricity cannot travel through the handle. How does this help to protect the electrician?

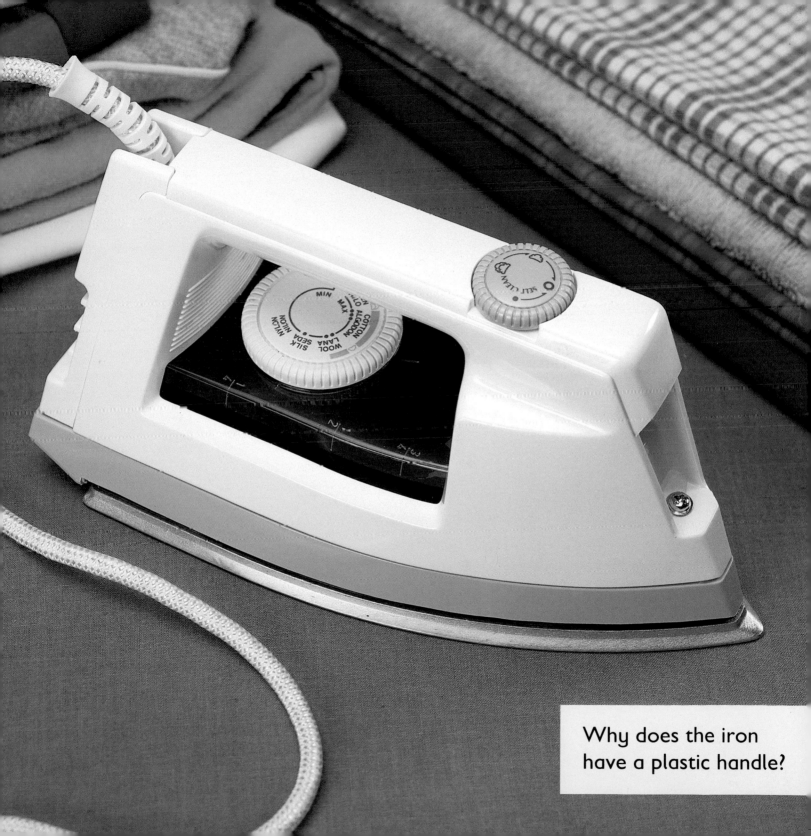

Why does the iron
have a plastic handle?

Plastic is a word
which describes an artificial material.
These pots are made from clay
dug from the earth.

These pots are made from plastic.
The plastic has been made
from chemicals found
in oil, gas and coal.

All kinds of things
are made using plastic ...

even some fabrics.

Plastics are used in many ways. This pan has a non-stick surface – made from plastic.

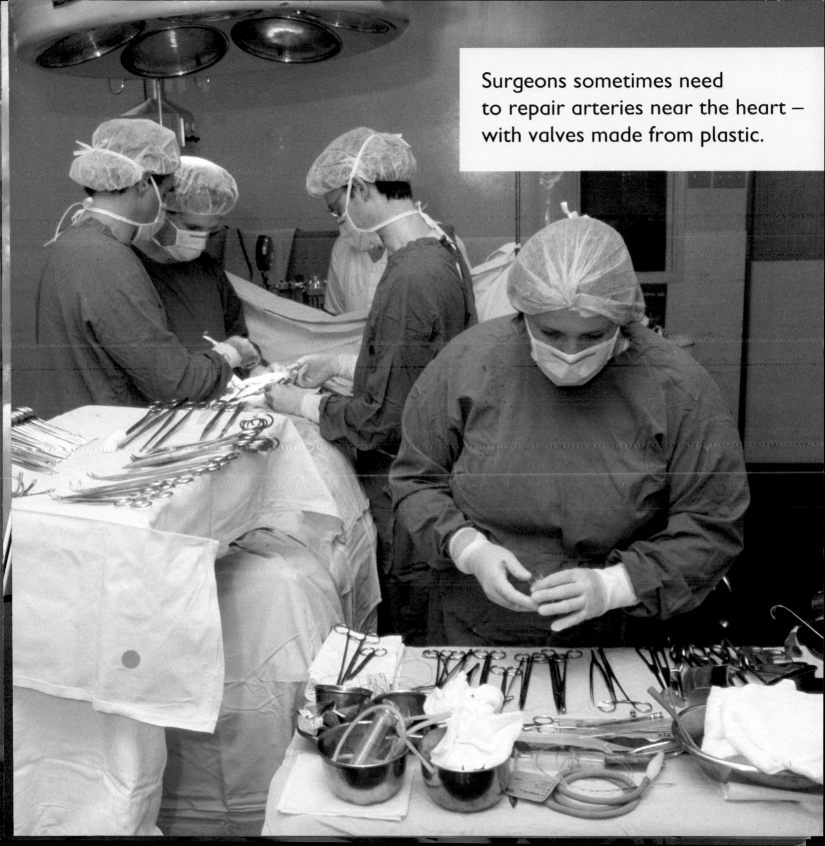

Surgeons sometimes need to repair arteries near the heart – with valves made from plastic.

Many glues, paints, toys,
scissors, cutlery, combs
pens and rulers
are made from plastic.

But materials like plastic
sometimes bring problems.
They are difficult to destroy.
What do we do
with all the plastic
we no longer need?

About this book

This book is designed for use in the home, kindergarten and infant school.

Parents can share the book with young children. Its aim is to bring into focus some of the elements of life and living which are all too often taken for granted. To develop fully, all young children need to have their understanding of the world deepened and the language they use to express their ideas extended. This book, and others in the series, takes the everyday things of the child's world and explores them, harnessing curiosity and wonder in a purposeful way.

For those working with young children each book is designed to be used both as a picture book, which explores ideas and concepts, and as a starting point to talk and exploration. The pictures have been selected because they are of interest in themselves and also because they include elements which will promote enquiry. Talk can lead to displays of items and pictures collected by children and teacher. Pictures and collages can be made by the children themselves.

Everything in our environment is of interest to the growing child. The purpose of these books is to extend and develop that interest.

Henry Pluckrose